ONWARD†

Biblical Beacons for the Christian Seeker's Journey

RC Atchisson

Printed in the United States of America

ISBN-10: 0-9864257-5-3
ISBN-13: 978-0-9864257-5-2

Stingy Brim LLC
St. Louis, MO 63123
www.rcatchisson.com

Cover Design by Jessica Sturgeon

All Scripture from the *King James Version of the Holy Bible, Old and New Testaments*

Names, characters, businesses, places, events and incidents are either the products of the author's imagination or used in a fictitious manner. Any resemblance to actual persons, living or dead, or actual events is purely coincidental.

Onward, Christian soldiers!
Marching as to war,
With the cross of Jesus
Going on before.
Christ, the royal Master,
Leads against the foe;
Forward into battle,
See his banners go!

Traditional Hymn,
Sabine Baring Gould
(1865)

Thy word is a lamp unto my feet, and a light unto my path.

--Psalm 119:105

Introduction

An old philosophical riddle asks "How far does one walk into a forest?" The answer to the brainteaser? "Only half way, because then he is walking out."

Semantic dexterity aside, there is a lot to be said for the theological implications of the puzzle. This crystalized when driving home one evening I saw an inspirational chestnut that pops up with stunning regularly on church signs everywhere. The familiar phrase simply asked "*If God seems farther away, who moved?*"

As a Christian, I hold the fundamental beliefs shared by other brothers and sisters in Christ. And, like all other persons of faith, I am a fallen person wholly dependent upon God's Grace and the sacrifice at Calvary. I fall short time and again only to find myself as befuddled as ever as to why the Lord would consent to call me home each time. Yet, each time, I am able to find my way home thanks to a Divinely-worded GPS, a codex that encapsulates the sum and substance of all that we are and all that we are called to be…*The Holy Bible.*

Still, the question remains. "Who moved?"

We live in a time when it is increasingly encouraged and celebrated to distance ourselves from God mentally, physically, and ultimately spiritually.

Our brains are bombarded with useless information at an astounding rate. We can cite box scores, movie quotes, and three out of four names of a given celebrity family with ease. But were we to be asked to quote more than odd line of Scripture by heart, how many of us would fail miserably in the attempt? Some polls report Church attendance is on the decline while others point out a dramatic recent drop in the number of people self-identifying as Christians. The result seems to be that the more God is out of our sight and the more He is off our mind, the less importance we place on Him.

Fortunately for us, He is always waiting right where we left Him. Even more fortunately for us, in addition to sending His son to atone for our sins, He makes certain that we can find Him…over and over again in some cases.

The *Onward!* series is a reminder of those lamps waiting to light our individual journeys be they our walk *to* God, *with* God, or *for* God. There are always those who will choose to walk *from* Him, but theirs is a journey marred by darkness and futility if for no other reason than they have chosen to walk away from the light and into the shadows.

The verses highlighted in this series were chosen for their relevance to the particular journey within which they appear. Arguably there are hundreds that could just as easily been inserted in their place. Still, the dozen passages that appear in each book are rich in both meaning and implication. That is why a list of questions to consider – or "Food for Thought" – will accompany each. These queries might already be at the lips, in the minds, or on the hearts of some as they read. Now they will be in black and white for serious consideration. My suggestion is to keep a dictionary nearby for things you don't get and those you don't want to forget.

Even more importantly, when considering the questions posed herein might I suggest that you look to some of the greatest minds in inspiration and apologetics today. Books by Billy Graham, C.S. Lewis and G.K. Chesterton are wonderful for filling the soul. Works from the likes of Ravi Zacharias, Eric Metexas, William Lane Craig, Peter Kreeft, and Lee Strobel are the perfect compliments in how they challenge the mind.

To be certain, the journey, at whichever stage one finds himself, will not be easy. It will tax us and test us at every turn. Still, in the end, we will find ourselves (*re-*)united with our Heavenly Father, no longer slaves to the darkness but awash in the Heaven glow of His Grace, His Mercy, and His Love.

Home sweet home, indeed.

How to Use This Workbook

Unlike most devotionals, this is designed to be read and considered at your own pace as opposed to "X" page or pages per day. In theory, each Scriptural verse is meant to be read, considered, and prayed over for a month. The exercises (*Paraphrasing, What it Means, Food for Thought*) are supplemental and meant to spur reflection and exploration. Do one a day, one every other day, or do them all and once and go back over them if you so choose.

As stated before, a Bible and a dictionary are recommended. Additionally, there are volumes upon volumes of scholarly consideration and apologetic works that make for wonderful reading and instruction.

The most important thing to remember about the task at hand is to remember that this is a personal journey. Where you find yourself today may not be where you find yourself tomorrow. In a perfect world, you will have progressed, but disappointment and obstacles are a part of life. Sometimes they knock us back a step. Sometimes they knock us off of our feet entirely. Sometimes the winds of ill fortune will force us to change course. The key is to remember the end goal – Our Heavenly Father.

Should a setback occur, do not give up. Dig deeper -- both into Scripture and into yourself. Read and re-read. Most importantly, pray. Ultimately, the Truth that is the Word of God will resonate. The beacons He has shared with us will light your path.

In either case, it is up to you to take those first steps…

The Seeker

The Journey *TO* God

Come unto me, all ye that labour and are heavy laden, and I will give you rest.

--Matthew 11:28

In the beginning God created the heaven and the earth.

-- Genesis 1:1

> **Quick Note:**
> *This isn't just the first line in the story; it is the basis for all that is to follow. In other words, you either believe this basic fact or there is no point in pretending to look toward anything else.*
> *Additionally, for those who are already people of faith, this is also ground zero – if you believe and accept this, then it makes no sense to cherry-pick throughout the rest of the Bible.*

Paraphrase

_____

_____

_____

_____

_____

Meaning

_____

_____

_____

_____

_____

_____

_____

_____

_____

Food for Thought

Creation or evolution? Does it make a difference? Why?

_____
_____
_____
_____
_____

What does creation mean?

_____
_____
_____
_____
_____

What does evolution mean?

_____
_____
_____
_____
_____

What is meant by Darwinian Evolution?

_____
_____
_____
_____
_____

Can science and religion co-exist?

_____
_____
_____
_____

Why do so many argue that it cannot?

_____
_____
_____
_____
_____

Who made God?

_____

_____

_____

_____

_____

What is meant by "Old Earth"? "New Earth"? How do they conflict or contradict?

_____

_____

_____

_____

_____

What is meant by "God of the gaps"?

_____

_____

_____

_____

_____

Should the Genesis account be taken literally?

_____

_____

_____

_____

_____

A*nd God said unto Moses, I Am That I Am: and he said, Thus shalt thou say unto the children of Israel, I Am hath sent me unto you.*

-- Exodus 3:14

> **Quick Note:**
> *Names were important to the Jewish people. Names denoted heritage, parentage, and even worked as a description. God's simple response leaves no room for doubt as to whom He is and the purpose He serves as beginning, middle, and end.*

Paraphrase

_____
_____
_____
_____
_____

Meaning

_____
_____
_____
_____
_____
_____
_____
_____
_____

Food for Thought

How do you picture God?

_____

_____

_____

_____

_____

How would/do you describe Him to others?

_____

_____

_____

_____

_____

What do you call Him (if anything)?

_____

_____

_____

_____

_____

What are the various names for God you have heard?

_____

_____

_____

_____

_____

What do the various names mean? What is their significance?

_____

_____

_____

_____

_____

Why is His name so important?

_____

_____

_____

_____

_____

What actually does it mean to take God's name in vain?

_____
_____
_____
_____
_____

Why is that such an offense?

_____
_____
_____
_____
_____

Why will Jews not write God's name?

_____
_____
_____
_____
_____

Which of His names seems most personally connective to you? Why?

_____
_____
_____
_____
_____

A*nd ye shall seek me, and find me, when ye shall search for me with all your heart.*

-- Jeremiah 29:13

Quick Note:
Though these words were originally spoken to the Jews, God's chosen people, during their 40 year travels in the desert, they are just as applicable today to those that seek God. And though we seek Him, no guarantees are made with regard to present miseries or obstacles being remedied. In fact, in seeking, we will discover that we are just a part of a much larger story.

Paraphrase

_____
_____
_____
_____
_____

Meaning

_____
_____
_____
_____
_____
_____
_____
_____
_____
_____

Food for Thought

How does someone "look" for God?

_____
_____
_____
_____
_____

What does it mean "with all your heart"?

_____
_____
_____
_____
_____

What are the implications of this promise?

_____
_____
_____
_____
_____

What is the Seeker's role in this implicit agreement?

_____
_____
_____
_____
_____

What problems might a Seeker face when first looking for God?

_____
_____
_____
_____

Can someone "find" God without looking? How so?

_____
_____
_____
_____

If someone is in the midst of turmoil and feels God "is not there", how might this verse be received by him or her?

_____
_____
_____
_____
_____

List some ways in which someone might seek God.

_____
_____
_____
_____
_____

What are some obstacles to seeking God.

_____
_____
_____
_____
_____

As a Seeker when will/would you know that you have "found" God?

_____
_____
_____
_____
_____

*T*he LORD *is my shepherd; I shall not want.*

He maketh me to lie down in green pastures: he leadeth me beside the still waters.

He restoreth my soul: he leadeth me in the paths of righteousness for his name's sake.

-- Psalm 23: 1-3

> **Quick Note:**
> *One of the most famous of all Psalms – in fact, one of the most famous of ALL Biblical verses, these lines serve to act as a comforting reminder that no matter where we find ourselves, we are not alone. Moreover, they serve to remind us that any and all we do his for Him...or, at least, should be.*

Paraphrase

_____
_____
_____
_____
_____

Meaning

_____
_____
_____
_____
_____
_____
_____
_____
_____
_____

Food for Thought

Share a time you would have gladly accepted the help of someone "shepherding" you through difficulty (ies).

_____

_____

_____

_____

_____

Does this verse provide a sense of comfort to you? Why? Why not?

_____

_____

_____

_____

_____

What times or events in your life do I recognize as "still waters"?

_____

_____

_____

_____

_____

What are your personal "green pastures"?

_____

_____

_____

_____

_____

When and why do you find your "still waters" and 'green pastures"?

_____

_____

_____

_____

_____

Was this psalm to be written by someone during a time of prosperity or hardship? Why?

_____

_____

_____

_____

_____

Who is the reputed author of this Psalm? How does that affect the reading? Meaning?

_____
_____
_____
_____
_____

What do you WANT right now? NEED? Describe the specific differences.

_____
_____
_____
_____
_____

What generally "restores" or replenishes you? Why?

_____
_____
_____
_____
_____

What scares you? Why?

_____
_____
_____
_____
_____

I know that, whatsoever God doeth, it shall be for ever: nothing can be put to it, nor any thing taken from it: and God doeth it, that men should fear before him.

-- Ecclesiastes 3:14

Paraphrase

_____
_____
_____
_____
_____

Meaning

_____
_____
_____
_____
_____
_____
_____
_____
_____
_____

Food for Thought

By what standard(s) could the world be considered "perfect"?

_____
_____
_____
_____
_____

What "imperfections" might some people recognize as a hindrance to the ideal described by Solomon?

_____
_____
_____
_____
_____

How might someone reconcile this "bad" being populated within the good of God's perfect creation?

_____
_____
_____
_____
_____

The most awe-inspiring thing you have ever seen is...

_____
_____
_____
_____
_____

For non-believers, this passage might require a true "leap of faith". Why/How so?

_____
_____
_____
_____

In what way does this passage require that the reader must a reader trust in God's plan?

_____
_____
_____
_____

How might a Seeker overcome doubts with regard to trusting God and His plan?

_____
_____
_____
_____
_____

How does God's perspective on time ("for ever") differ from that of man?

_____
_____
_____
_____
_____

In what sense does Solomon mean we should "fear" God?

_____
_____
_____
_____
_____

If all God has done is perfect, what affect can man have on it?

_____
_____
_____
_____
_____

*A*fter this manner therefore pray ye: Our Father which art in heaven, Hallowed be thy name.

Thy kingdom come, Thy will be done in earth, as it is in heaven.

Give us this day our daily bread.

And forgive us our debts, as we forgive our debtors.

And lead us not into temptation, but deliver us from evil: For thine is the kingdom, and the power, and the glory, for ever. Amen.

--Matthew 6: 9-13

> **Quick Note:**
> *Known by a variety of names names – the Lord's Prayer, the Perfect Prayer, the Pater Noster – the Our Father is the template handed down to us by Jesus himself as the way in which we should pray.*

Paraphrase

_____
_____
_____
_____
_____

Meaning

_____
_____
_____
_____
_____
_____
_____
_____
_____
_____

Food for Thought

What is important about the way Jesus suggests we address God?

_____

_____

_____

_____

_____

Identify the seven requests the prayer makes of God:

_____

_____

_____

_____

_____

Why is God's name important to be revered ("hallowed")?

_____

_____

_____

_____

_____

What does "Thy kingdom come" mean?

_____

_____

_____

_____

_____

For what are we asking when we pray "Your will be done in earth, as it is in heaven"?

_____

_____

_____

_____

Explain the importance of our needing to "forgive our debtors".

_____

_____

_____

_____

_____

Does God actually "lead" us into temptation?

_____

_____

_____

_____

_____

In what way can/does God deliver us from specific evils?

_____

_____

_____

_____

_____

What is important about the doxology ("For thine is the kingdom, and the power, and the glory for ever") at the end?

_____

_____

_____

_____

_____

How does the prayer, in its entirety, serve to glorify God?

_____

_____

_____

_____

_____

When Jesus heard it, he saith unto them, They that are whole have no need of the physician, but they that are sick: I came not to call the righteous, but sinners to repentance.

-- Mark 2:17

> **Quick Note:**
> *Jesus gave the first, best sense of His mission with this response to a question that the Pharisees and Scribes had but failed to address with Him directly.*

Paraphrase

_____
_____
_____
_____
_____

Meaning

_____
_____
_____
_____
_____
_____
_____
_____
_____
_____

Food for Thought

What is sin?

_____
_____
_____
_____
_____

Is sin something we bring upon ourselves? Why? Why not?

_____
_____
_____
_____
_____

How is sin like a disease?

_____
_____
_____
_____
_____

What is significant about Christ's answer?

_____
_____
_____
_____
_____

Of what significance is the meaning of the word "Pharisee" to the story?

_____
_____
_____
_____
_____

Why might someone avoid visiting a doctor? When and why have you?

_____
_____
_____
_____
_____

How do we typically view/respond to sinners?

_____
_____
_____
_____

If we are all broken sinners, how is this passage an encouragement?

_____
_____
_____
_____

Who does Jesus suggest are actually the "sick" in this scenario?

_____
_____
_____
_____

In what ways might a Seeker "be healed"?

_____
_____
_____
_____

***F**or God so loved the world, that he gave his only begotten Son, that whosoever believeth in him should not perish, but have everlasting life.*

-- John 3:16

> **Quick Note:**
> *The continuation of Jesus' discussion with Nicodemus is possibly the single most important verse of the Bible for a Seeker and the basis of our journey as believers. Without acknowledging or accepting this, the entire search is for naught.*

Paraphrase

_____
_____
_____
_____
_____

Meaning

_____
_____
_____
_____
_____
_____
_____
_____
_____

Food for Thought

According to this verse, how did God illustrate His love for us?

_____
_____
_____
_____
_____

What is the importance of this act? How does the world benefit?

_____
_____
_____
_____
_____

What is the promise of this passage?

_____
_____
_____
_____
_____

Why might a Seeker fail to recognize God's love?

_____
_____
_____
_____
_____

What are the characteristics you recognize in someone who is loved by another?

_____
_____
_____
_____

Why might a Seeker feel unloved by God?

_____
_____
_____
_____

When/How might a Seeker recognize God's love?

_____
_____
_____
_____
_____

If we accept God's love, then what responsibility(ies) do we have?

_____
_____
_____
_____
_____

How might this passage be misunderstood or misinterpreted?

_____
_____
_____
_____
_____

What is Jesus' role in the world?

_____
_____
_____
_____
_____

S tand fast therefore in the liberty wherewith Christ hath made us free, and be not entangled again with the yoke of bondage.

-- Galatians 5:1

> **Quick Note:**
> *A consistent mischaracterization of Christianity is that it is defined by constraints and limits. However, this verse illustrates that the opposite is true. The defining characterization of the Christian faith for all, whether they believe themselves to be searching or those who profess to have found, is liberty – freedom from sin and freedom from death.*

Paraphrase

_____
_____
_____
_____
_____

Meaning

_____
_____
_____
_____
_____
_____
_____
_____
_____
_____

Food for Thought

What does "liberty" mean in this context?

_____
_____
_____
_____
_____

How did Christ make us free?

_____
_____
_____
_____
_____

What imagery is invoked by the word choice at the end of the verse?

_____
_____
_____
_____
_____

In what ways is the imagery appropriate?

_____
_____
_____
_____
_____

Are we able to free ourselves? Why? Why not?

_____
_____
_____
_____
_____

What are we told to do? Why is the phrasing important to our understanding of this passage?

_____
_____
_____
_____
_____

What is the extent of our freedom in Christ?

_____
_____
_____
_____
_____

Do we have any newfound responsibility to earn or keep this freedom? Explain.

_____
_____
_____
_____
_____

From what bondage would you like to free yourself?

_____
_____
_____
_____
_____

How do you envision yourself as "free"?

_____
_____
_____
_____
_____

For by grace are ye saved through faith; and that not of yourselves: it is the gift of God:

Not of works, lest any man should boast.

--Ephesians 2: 8-9

> **Quick Note:**
> *This – along with James 2 (24,26) – is one of the primary causes of the schism between Catholics and Protestants. Wherever one falls down on that discussion, one important detail emerges – God has gifted us with His grace.*

Paraphrase

_____
_____
_____
_____
_____

Meaning

_____
_____
_____
_____
_____
_____
_____
_____
_____
_____

Food for Thought

According to Paul, the author, what elements are the keys to our salvation?

_____
_____
_____
_____
_____

What is meant by "grace"?

_____
_____
_____
_____
_____

What is meant by "faith"?

_____
_____
_____
_____
_____

What is meant by "saved"?

_____
_____
_____
_____
_____

What is a gift you have received simply because someone loved you enough to give it to you? How is that similar to the assertion that Paul makes about God's gift to us?

_____
_____
_____
_____

According to this verse, what is our role in our own salvation?

_____
_____
_____
_____
_____

In what are we fore-warned by implication to not indulge? Why?

_____
_____
_____
_____
_____

What are the differences between Catholics and Protestants on this point?

_____
_____
_____
_____
_____

On what points to they agree? Disagree?

_____
_____
_____
_____
_____

Can this difference be reconciled? Should it be? Does it need to be?

_____
_____
_____
_____
_____

*A*ll Scripture is given by inspiration of God, and is profitable for doctrine, for reproof, for correction, for instruction in righteousness, that the man of God may be complete, thoroughly equipped for every good work.

-- 2 Timothy 3:16-17

Quick Note:
Often, people will dispute the necessity and even the veracity of the Bible itself. This verse tackles both. It addresses why people of faith put such stock in the Word. Even more importantly, these verses list the ways in which a Seeker can successfully utilize all that is contained therein—for his or her own good and for the good of the world at large.

Paraphrase

_____
_____
_____
_____
_____

Meaning

_____
_____
_____
_____
_____
_____
_____
_____
_____
_____

Food for Thought

According to the author of these verses, from where did all Scripture originate?

_____
_____
_____
_____
_____

What is meant by "inspiration"?

_____
_____
_____
_____
_____

What three purposes does Scripture serve?

_____
_____
_____
_____
_____

In what ways is Scripture seen as "profitable"?

_____
_____
_____
_____
_____

Ultimately, Scripture equips us for what?

_____
_____
_____
_____

Without Scripture, the author implies that a Seeker is what? Do you believe the author of this verse is correct? Why / Why not?

_____
_____
_____
_____

What do you envision God's role to be during this process?

_____
_____
_____
_____
_____

Why do you think so many people have such a problem with Biblical Authority?

_____
_____
_____
_____
_____

What, if anything, could change the opinion of someone who denies the authority of Scripture? Why?

_____
_____
_____
_____
_____

What would you say to someone who says there are too many versions and too much has been lost in translation?

_____
_____
_____
_____
_____

***N*ow faith is the substance of things hoped for, the evidence of things not seen.**

For by it the elders obtained a good report.

Through faith we understand that the worlds were framed by the word of God, so that things which are seen were not made of things which do appear.

--Hebrews 11:1-3

Quick Note:
This passage is both highly important and extremely challenging. Its importance lies in the fact that it suggests the frame of mind in which we must find ourselves to seek, and ultimately find, God. Its challenge lies in that self-same frame of mind.

Paraphrase

_____
_____
_____
_____
_____

Meaning

_____
_____
_____
_____
_____
_____
_____
_____
_____
_____

Food for Thought

What does "faith" mean to you?

_____
_____
_____
_____
_____

What is the dictionary definition of "faith"?

_____
_____
_____
_____
_____

How do your definition, the dictionary definition, and this verse look when compared side by side?

_____
_____
_____
_____
_____

What is the author of this verse saying about the things we can see?

_____
_____
_____
_____
_____

What is meant by "For by it the elders obtained a good report"?

_____
_____
_____
_____
_____

What might be some of the "things not seen" referred to in the first verse?

_____
_____
_____
_____
_____

What difficulty might a Seeker have with these "things unseen"?

_____

_____

_____

_____

_____

How could he or she come to terms with them?

_____

_____

_____

_____

_____

What is your biggest difficulty with the concept of "faith"?

_____

_____

_____

_____

_____

How do you/could you reconcile that difficulty? Will/Have you? Why? Why not?

_____

_____

_____

_____

_____

The grace of our Lord Jesus Christ be with you all. Amen.

-- Revelation 22:21

Living Water

Did you know that almost 800 million people worldwide lack access to clean drinking water?

To date, Living Water International has completed over 15,000 water projects in 26 countries. Just by purchasing this book you have already helped them in their efforts as 10% of all profits are being donated, but I hope you would consider additional support – either individually or with the help of an organization or community to which you belong.

For more information about the great folks at Living Water International and their mission, please visit www.water.cc .

About the Author

RC Atchisson is a Midwest native, born and raised in St. Louis, Missouri. A teacher for almost 20 years, he has written for print, radio, television, and film. In addition, he has produced a variety of independent and live theatrical projects.

www.ingramcontent.com/pod-product-compliance
Lightning Source LLC
Chambersburg PA
CBHW080217040426
42331CB00036B/3272